WELCOME TO MY COUNTRY

Welcome to
VIETNAM

Gareth Stevens Publishing
A WORLD ALMANAC EDUCATION GROUP COMPANY

Written by
YUMI NG/AMY CONDRA-PETERS

Edited in USA by
DOROTHY L. GIBBS

Designed by
GEOSLYN LIM

Picture research by
SUSAN JANE MANUEL

First published in North America in 2003 by
Gareth Stevens Publishing
A World Almanac Education Group Company
330 West Olive Street, Suite 100
Milwaukee, Wisconsin 53212 USA

Please visit our web site at:
www.garethstevens.com
For a free color catalog describing
Gareth Stevens' list of high-quality
books and multimedia programs,
call 1-800-542-2595 (USA) or
1-800-387-3178 (CANADA).
Gareth Stevens Publishing's fax: (414) 332-3567.

© **TIMES MEDIA PRIVATE LIMITED 2003**
Originated and designed by
Times Editions
An imprint of Times Media Private Limited
A member of the Times Publishing Group
Times Centre, 1 New Industrial Road
Singapore 536196
http://www.timesone.com.sg/te

Library of Congress Cataloging-in-Publication Data
Ng, Yumi.
Welcome to Vietnam / Yumi Ng and Amy Condra-Peters.
p. cm. — (Welcome to my country)
Summary: An introduction to the geography, history, government,
economy, people, and culture of Vietnam.
Includes bibliographical references and index.
ISBN 0-8368-2548-9 (lib. bdg.)
1. Vietnam—Juvenile literature. [1. Vietnam.]
I. Condra-Peters, Amy. II. Title. III. Series.
DS556.3.N4   2003
959.7—dc21   2002030284

Printed in Malaysia

1 2 3 4 5 6 7 8 9 07 06 05 04 03

PICTURE CREDITS
Allsport/Stanley Chou: 36
ANA Press Agency/Jean Rey: 32 (top)
Art Directors and Trip Photo Library: 17, 23
Michele Burgess: 29, 40 (both)
Camera Press: 31
Embassy of the Socialist Republic
    of Vietnam: 15 (bottom)
Ron Emmons: 34, 35
Alain Evrard: 3 (center), 5, 24, 45
Getty Images/HultonArchive: 15 (top)
HBL Network Photo Agency: 1, 3 (bottom),
    7 (bottom)
Dave G. Houser: 32 (bottom)
The Hutchison Library: cover, 4, 6, 7 (top),
    11, 18, 19, 22, 25, 27 (bottom), 38
John R. Jones: 9 (top), 33, 37
Björn Klingwall: 28
North Wind Picture Archive: 12
Christine Osborne: 3 (top), 30
Photobank Photolibrary: 9 (bottom), 10
Topham Picturepoint: 13, 14, 16, 39, 41
Travel Ink/Colin Marshall: 2
Marc Wang/Ng Lay San: 44 (both)
Alison Wright: 8, 20, 21, 26, 27 (top)

Digital Scanning by Superskill Graphics Pte Ltd

Contents

Words that appear in the glossary are printed in **boldface** type the first time they occur in the text.

Welcome to Vietnam!

Vietnam is a long, narrow country in Southeast Asia. For hundreds of years, it was controlled by the Chinese. Then the French took control. The country was divided into North Vietnam and South Vietnam from 1954 until 1976, when it united to form the Socialist Republic of Vietnam. Let's visit this republic and learn about its people.

Opposite: These boys in Ho Chi Minh City, which used to be called Saigon, enjoy flying kites.

Below: Qui Nhon has a large seaside fish market where people buy and sell fresh seafood.

The Flag of Vietnam

Vietnam's flag is bright red with one big, yellow star in the center. The star's five points represent the country's farmers, workers, **intellectuals**, youth, and soldiers.

The Land

Vietnam has an area of 127,243 square miles (329,560 square kilometers) and is shaped like the letter *S*. Its neighbors are China to the north and Laos and Cambodia to the west. The country's long eastern coastline is on the Gulf of Tonkin in the north and on the South China Sea in the south. The Gulf of Thailand is on the southwestern coast.

Below: Highland areas in Vietnam have many forests, streams, and waterfalls.

Most of Vietnam is covered with hills and mountains. At 10,312 feet (3,143 meters), Mount Fan Si Pan, in the northwestern Fan Si Pan-Sa Phin mountain range, is Vietnam's highest peak. Annamese Cordillera, along the coast, is another important range.

Important rivers include the Red River in northern Vietnam and the Mekong River in southern Vietnam. Both start in China and flow across Vietnam to the sea. The Mekong is the longest river in Southeast Asia.

Above: The port city of Nha Trang, on the South China Sea, has beautiful, sandy beaches.

Below: Hundreds of islands and thousands of caves attract millions of visitors each year to Ha Long Bay.

Climate

In northern Vietnam, the hot summer months last from May through October. During this time, heavy rainfall and **typhoons** are common. November through April is the dry winter season.

Tropical southern Vietnam has its hottest weather from February to May. Its coolest period is November through January. Heavy rains usually begin in May and can last until November.

Above:
These women are working in the rice fields of northern Vietnam. Rice is planted during the warm, wet summer months in northern areas and during the rainy season in southern areas.

Plants and Animals

Teak and rare dwarf bamboo are two of thousands of plant species in the forests of Vietnam. The forests are also a rich source of food, medicine, and **timber**.

Vietnam has thousands of animal species, too, including tigers, leopards, bears, Indian elephants, rhinoceroses, and crocodiles. Some of Asia's rarest animals, such as the Vu Quang ox and the giant muntjac, also live there.

Above: Orchids are one of many kinds of flowering plants in Vietnam.

Left: Like many other kinds of animals in Vietnam, Indian elephants are in danger of becoming extinct.

9

History

Modern Vietnamese are believed to be descendants of the Viet and the Dong Son peoples. Both were rice farmers living in the northern Vietnam region around 1000 B.C.

The Chinese conquered this region in the second century B.C. and named it Annam. They ruled until A.D. 939. From the Chinese, the Vietnamese learned farming methods, fine arts, and **Confucianism**. The Chinese took control of the region again in 1407.

Left:
The architecture of the Pavilion of Splendor, located in Hue, shows the influence of Chinese design.

Left: The tomb of Emperor Khai Dinh took eleven years to build. It is located near Hue. Khai Dinh, of the Nguyen dynasty, reigned from 1916 to 1925.

A Vietnamese landowner named Le Loi defeated the Chinese in 1428. He became Emperor Le Thai To, and his **dynasty** eventually conquered all of Vietnam. Two families, however, governed the country. The Trinh family ruled in the north. The Nguyen family controlled the south and central parts.

In the 1770s, the Tay Son family rebelled and took control from both the Trinhs and the Nguyens. Then, in 1802, a Nguyen named Gia Long, with help from the French army, defeated the Tay Sons and became emperor.

French Rule

Emperor Gia Long allowed French **merchants** and Catholic missionaries to live and work in Vietnam, but the next emperor, Minh Mang, **persecuted** them. In 1859, the French fought back by capturing Saigon, which is now Ho Chi Minh City. In 1862, other regions in the south came under French rule, forming the colony of Cochinchina. Forced to pay taxes to the French, the Vietnamese became resentful.

Above:
In this illustration, French troops, in 1885, are capturing the town of Lang Son, in northern Vietnam.

Independence and War

When World War II ended in 1945, Ho Chi Minh, a **nationalist** leader, and his **communist** group, the Viet Minh, took control of northern Vietnam. Ho Chi Minh declared Vietnam's independence, but the French tried to take back control. The Viet Minh defeated the French in the First Indochina War (1946–1954). Then, Ngo Dinh Diem, a Catholic who had served in the Nguyen royal court, established the Republic of Vietnam, or South Vietnam. In 1963, the Viet Cong overthrew Diem, starting the Second Indochina War, or Vietnam War. North Vietnam won this war in 1975.

Left: Ngo Dinh Diem, shown here with his family (*back row, second from left*), named himself president of South Vietnam. His government was taken over by the Viet Cong, a communist group in the south that was supported by North Vietnam.

The Socialist Republic of Vietnam

In 1976, North and South Vietnam united, forming the Socialist Republic of Vietnam. Because the republic's communist government imprisoned people who had different political **views**, thousands of Vietnamese **fled** the country.

When Vietnamese communists invaded Cambodia in 1978, the United States and other countries stopped trade with Vietnam until its troops withdrew from Cambodia.

Below:
Vietnamese troops left Cambodia in 1989. The United States started to trade with Vietnam again in 1994.

The Trung Sisters (?–A.D. 43)

In A.D. 40, sisters Trung Trac and Trung Nhi rode elephants as they led Vietnamese forces in driving the Chinese out of Vietnam. In A.D. 43, the Chinese recaptured the country. Legend says that the Trung sisters drowned themselves in a river to avoid surrendering to the Chinese.

Ho Chi Minh

Ho Chi Minh (1890–1969)

His real name was Nguyen Sinh Cung. *Ho Chi Minh* means "he who enlightens." Ho Chi Minh was the founder of the Communist Party in Vietnam and was president of the Democratic Republic of Vietnam (North Vietnam) from 1945 to 1969.

Nguyen Thi Binh

Nguyen Thi Binh (1927–)

In 1969, Nguyen Thi Binh, a former teacher, became South Vietnam's minister of foreign affairs. Since 1992, she has been Vietnam's vice president.

Government and the Economy

The Communist Party of Vietnam rules the Socialist Republic of Vietnam. It is the country's only political party. The fifteen-member Political Bureau, or Politburo, decides government **policy**, and the country's prime minister is the head of government.

Below: Built in the early 1900s, the Presidential Palace in Hanoi, Vietnam's capital city, has a British style of architecture.

TOÀN ĐẢNG
TOÀN QUÂN
TOÀN DÂN

KIÊN ĐỊNH ĐI THEO CON ĐƯỜNG CỦA ĐẢNG VÀ BÁC HỒ ĐÃ CHỌN

Left: Images of Ho Chi Minh appear on banners, posters, and billboards all over Vietnam. He is often called the father of Vietnam because of his dedicated fight to unite the country.

A 450-member National Assembly represents the Vietnamese people. It elects the prime minister as well as the president, vice president, and other key officials. The Supreme People's Court is the highest court in Vietnam's justice system.

Vietnam has fifty-seven provinces and four **municipalities**. The provinces are divided into smaller units, each of which elects a local People's Council. All Vietnamese citizens eighteen years and older must vote in every election.

Economic Changes

After the Vietnam War, the country's economy had many problems. In 1986, the Vietnamese government began to make economic reforms. The changes allowed farmers to decide which crops to grow and how to sell them. They also allowed families to run their own small businesses. By the early 1990s, Vietnam's economy was one of the fastest-growing in the world, and life for the Vietnamese was improving.

Above:
To produce more energy for Vietnam, the Vietnamese government built this hydroelectric dam near Da Lat.

Agriculture and Exports

Growing rice is the most important agricultural activity in Vietnam. The nation is the world's second-largest exporter of rice, after Thailand. It is the third-largest exporter of coffee, after Brazil and Colombia.

Vietnam also exports tea, rubber, textiles, shoes, oil, marine products, and handicrafts, trading mostly with Japan, China, South Korea, Taiwan, Singapore, and France.

Below: Large containers loaded with imports and exports come into and go out of the port at Haiphong, which is on the Gulf of Tonkin.

People and Lifestyle

With more than eighty million people, including at least fifty **ethnic groups**, Vietnam is one of the most populated nations in the world.

Hill groups, such as the Hmong, Muong, Nung, and Tay, make up about 10 percent of the country's population. Other groups include the Khmer and the Cham. The Khmer, of Cambodian descent, live near Cambodia, and the

Left: Vietnamese parents teach their children obedience, honor, and respect. When his baby daughter grows up, this father will expect her to take care of him.

Cham are descendants of the Champa kingdom that once ruled the central coast of Vietnam. Approximately two million ethnic Chinese, known as the Hoa, also live in Vietnam, mostly in southern provinces.

Above: These girls are Hmongs, one of the hill groups living in Vietnam's northern and central highlands.

Gracious People

Vietnamese culture values dignity and politeness, so its people try not to show strong emotions in public.

Family Life

In a Vietnamese family, grandparents, parents, aunts, uncles, and children often live together in one house. Every working family member is expected to contribute part of his or her earnings to help with the household expenses.

The Vietnamese have great respect for the elderly. Because they believe their ancestors continue to live after death, they make **offerings** to the spirits of their close relatives on the anniversaries of their deaths.

Above: Many people in Vietnam use bicycles and motorcycles to get around. Young children often ride with their parents.

Women in Vietnam

Vietnamese culture expects women to be **submissive** daughters and wives, yet they still have a say in family decisions. Besides doing most of the household chores, Vietnamese women have jobs in rice fields, factories, or offices.

Below: These young newlyweds are posing for a photograph with family members right after their wedding in Ho Chi Minh City.

In the Socialist Republic of Vietnam, men and women have equal rights, but most women still have low-paying jobs. The Vietnamese Women's Union lends money to women to help them set up and run small businesses.

Education

The government of Vietnam has been very successful in providing at least basic education to the country's people. More than 90 percent of the population can read and write, and all children attend primary school.

Primary school in Vietnam lasts five years. Lower secondary school lasts four years. Some students then go on to upper secondary school for three years.

Below: Primary schoolboys in Ho Chi Minh City sometimes meet with friends on the street after school.

Most rural areas have only one-room schoolhouses and not enough teachers. Many children in these areas stop attending after primary school to help their families by working in the fields or markets.

A university education in Vietnam usually lasts four years. Today, about 500,000 students attend. The most respected university in the country is the National University of Hanoi.

Above: These girls in Hanoi are happy to be celebrating their graduation day from upper secondary school. A few graduates will go on to a university.

Religion

Vietnam has six official religions: Buddhism, Roman Catholicism, Protestantism, Islam, the Hoa Hao faith, and the Cao Dai faith.

Most Vietnamese are Buddhists. Buddhism is an ancient religion that was introduced in Vietnam in the second century. Buddhists believe that life is a **cycle** of birth, death, and rebirth and that actions in the present life decide the quality of the next life.

Roman Catholicism was brought to Vietnam by Europeans in the sixteenth century and became a major religion there when the country was ruled by the French. Missionaries from North America introduced Protestantism in the nineteenth and twentieth centuries. Arab traders brought Islam to Vietnam in the seventh century. Hoa Hao, which is a simpler form of Buddhism, started in Vietnam in the twentieth century.

Above: Cao Dai is a mixture of Taoist, Buddhist, Islamic, Christian, and Confucian beliefs. Its symbol, the all-seeing Divine Eye, represents God.

Language

Most of the people in Vietnam speak Vietnamese. Modern Vietnamese is **monosyllabic** and has a complicated set of **tones**.

The **script** of written Vietnamese, which first appeared between the ninth and the eleventh centuries, is based on Chinese characters. In the 1200s, a new written form developed, using the Vietnamese pronunciation of Chinese characters. In the 1600s, French priest Alexandre de Rhodes created a written form using the Latin alphabet.

Left: In written Vietnamese, special symbols above letters in the words show which of the language's six tones should be used when the words are spoken.

Above:
Newsstands, like this one in Ho Chi Minh City, sell a variety of books, newspapers, and magazines.

Literature

Classical Chinese poetry influenced the first Vietnamese writings, which appeared in about the tenth century. In the 1930s, French authors inspired the Vietnamese to write **prose**. Modern Vietnamese authors usually write about daily life. The communist government must approve the content of all books and magazines published in Vietnam.

Arts

For centuries, China's artistic traditions have influenced the art of Vietnam. Vietnamese artists often have dragons, unicorns, and other **mythical** creatures in their paintings and carvings.

In ancient times, Vietnamese artists used **bronze** to create Chinese-style drums as well as statues of gods and mythical animals. Cham artists carved beautiful figures out of sandstone.

Below: Cham architecture had a graceful style and included many elaborately decorated Hindu towers. Some of the towers built along Vietnam's central coastline are still standing.

Painting

Traditionally, Vietnam's artists painted only on silk. Then, in 1925, the French founded an art school in Hanoi, where Vietnamese artists learned European techniques. Nguyen Sang, Nguyen Tu Ngheim, and Bui Xuan Phai are great Vietnamese painters from that school who inspired new artists to combine Western and Asian styles and methods.

Above:
The Mekong River, painted in 1993, is the work of Vietnamese artist Hoang Lan Anh.

Traditional Crafts

Mother-of-pearl **inlay** is a craft that has been practiced in Vietnam for a thousand years. It is used to decorate cabinets, chests, and other furniture items. Embroidery and pottery are also traditional crafts. Dragons, butterflies, and Chinese characters are some of the designs stitched onto silk or velvet clothing and cushion covers. Animal figures have been popular pottery designs since the fifteenth century.

Above: The art of water puppetry started in northern Vietnam. Modern puppeteers still use the techniques developed by Red River area farmers as early as 1121.

Music and Opera

Traditional Vietnamese music is played on instruments such as bamboo flutes and xylophones and single-stringed lutes, as well as on gongs and drums. It uses the same five-note musical scale as traditional Chinese music.

Traditional *cheo* (chay-oh) opera, which combines song, dance, poetry, and mime, is Vietnam's oldest form of theater. Classical *tuong* (toong) opera came to Vietnam from China in the 1300s. Modern *cai luong* (kye loong) opera began in Vietnam in 1920.

Left: The Nghia Binh Classical Opera Society performs tuong operas in the province of Binh Dinh. The actors in tuong dramas wear elaborate costumes and heavy makeup.

Leisure

In Vietnam's cities, people like to relax in the parks. Men often get together in cafés to talk and play cards or games such as chess and Chinese checkers. Most Vietnamese enjoy movies. They watch films from Western countries as well as those produced in Vietnam. Kung fu movies are especially popular. The Vietnamese also enjoy **karaoke**.

Below: Especially in the evenings and on weekends, groups of friends like to meet for a stroll in Vietnam's shady parks.

Activities for Children

Vietnamese cities have many activities for children, including sports and the arts. Some children attend dance, music, or martial arts classes that are held after school. Youth centers offer plays, magic shows, and water puppet performances.

Most Vietnamese girls and boys like to ride bicycles, jump rope, swim, read comic books, and play games. *Da cau* (dah cow) is a favorite children's game in Vietnam.

Above: These young artists are practicing their painting at Lenin Park in Hanoi.

Sports

The Vietnamese are good swimmers, bowlers, and badminton, table tennis (Ping-Pong), volleyball, and soccer players. Soccer has a huge following in Vietnam. Regional tournaments held in Hanoi and Ho Chi Minh City attract thousands of enthusiastic fans. Thousands also watch World Cup soccer on television. In the future, Vietnam hopes to compete more in international soccer events.

Above: Vietnam's Nguyen Hong Son tries to score a goal in a soccer match against Cambodia that was played in Thailand in 2000.

Martial Arts

In 1938, Nguyen Loc created a form of martial arts, called Vovinam, that develops endurance, strength, and speed. In 1964, "Vovinam" became "Vovinam-Viet Vo Dao," or "The Philosophy of Vietnamese Martial Arts," and rapidly became popular in many parts of the world. The Vietnamese have a strong interest in martial arts. Kung fu and karate are two other popular forms.

Below: Early in the morning, some Vietnamese get together outdoors to practice the slow movements of tai chi, a type of ancient Chinese exercise.

National Holidays

Independence Day, on September 2, is the most important national holiday in Vietnam. It celebrates Ho Chi Minh's declaration of Vietnam's independence in 1945. Liberation Day, on April 30, celebrates the day in 1975 when North Vietnamese forces united the country.

Above: At Mid-Autumn Festival time, Vietnam's shops are filled with brightly colored lanterns that are shaped like animals and other objects.

Opposite: These children are waiting on a street in Ho Chi Minh City for the Independence Day parade.

Wandering Souls Day

One of the most important festivals in Vietnam each year is held to honor family members who have died. On Wandering Souls Day, living family members pray and make offerings, either at home or at a temple.

Mid-Autumn Festival

Children, in particular, enjoy Vietnam's Mid-Autumn Festival, which is held in September. During the festival, they are given colorful lanterns shaped like dragons, butterflies, and other figures. In the evening, they parade through the streets with their lanterns.

Food

Vietnamese food combines Chinese, Thai, Indonesian, and French cooking methods and ingredients, but popular dishes are different in the country's three regions. Dishes in the southern region use fresh herbs and tropical fruits, such as coconuts, pineapples, and papayas. Seafood dishes are popular in the central coastal region. Cooking in the northern region is like Chinese, and dishes are often stir-fried.

Above: Durians are one kind of tropical fruit that grows in Vietnam. Although the shell is thorny, the fruit is soft and creamy.

Left: Vendors on the roads in Ho Chi Minh City sell many different foods, both cooked and uncooked.

Above: This group of friends has gathered for dinner at a restaurant in Ho Chi Minh City.

People in Vietnam eat rice three times a day. They dish up the rice into small bowls, then add vegetables and meats. *Pho* (fuh) is a common dish. It is noodle soup made with fresh herbs and served with chicken, pork, or beef. *Cha gio* (chah yaw), a crispy eggroll stuffed with noodles, pork, garlic, and other foods, is popular for snacks. Common seasonings include fish sauce, shrimp paste, and chili peppers.

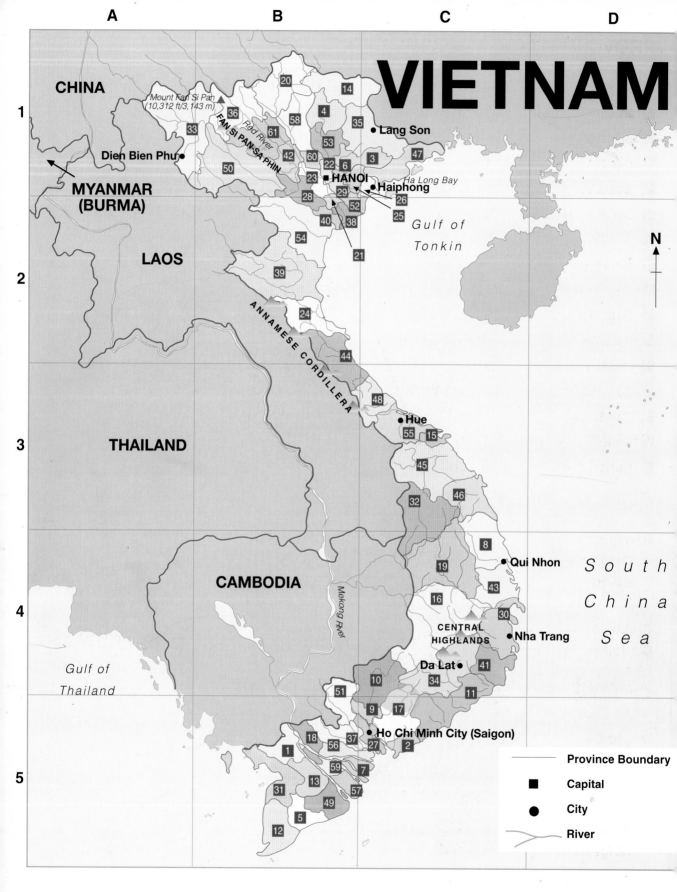

VIETNAM

CHINA

1

Mount Fan Si Pan
(10,312 ft/3,143 m)

20

14

36

4

33

58

35

• Lang Son

Red River

61

53

FAN SI PAN-SA PHIN

42

60

3

47

Dien Bien Phu •

50

22

6

23

■ **HANOI**

Ha Long Bay

**MYANMAR
(BURMA)**

28

29

• Haiphong

26

52

25

40

38

*Gulf of
Tonkin*

LAOS

54

21

N

2

39

24

ANNAMESE CORDILLERA

44

THAILAND

48

• Hue

55

15

3

45

32

46

8

19

• Qui Nhon

South

CAMBODIA

43

16

China

Mekong River

30

**CENTRAL
HIGHLANDS**

• Nha Trang

Sea

4

Da Lat •

41

34

11

10

51

9

17

2

18

37

• Ho Chi Minh City (Saigon)

56

27

1

59

7

*Gulf of
Thailand*

31

13

57

49

5

12

5

	Province Boundary
■	Capital
●	City
	River

42

PROVINCES AND *MUNICIPALITIES

1 An Giang
2 Ba Ria-Vung Tau
3 Bac Giang
4 Bac Kan
5 Bac Lieu
6 Bac Ninh
7 Ben Tre
8 Binh Dinh
9 Binh Duong
10 Binh Phuoc
11 Binh Thuan
12 Ca Mau
13 Can Tho
14 Cao Bang
15 * Da Nang
16 Dac Lac

17 Dong Nai
18 Dong Thap
19 Gia Lai
20 Ha Giang
21 Ha Nam
22 * Ha Noi
23 Ha Tay
24 Ha Tinh
25 Hai Duong
26 * Hai Phong
27 * Ho Chi Minh
28 Hoa Binh
29 Hung Yen
30 Khanh Hoa
31 Kien Giang
32 Kon Tum

33 Lai Chau
34 Lam Dong
35 Lang Son
36 Lao Cai
37 Long An
38 Nam Dinh
39 Nghe An
40 Ninh Binh
41 Ninh Thuan
42 Phu Tho
43 Phu Yen
44 Quang Binh
45 Quang Nam
46 Quang Ngai
47 Quang Ninh
48 Quang Tri

49 Soc Trang
50 Son La
51 Tay Ninh
52 Thai Binh
53 Thai Nguyen
54 Thanh Hoa
55 Thua Thien-Hue
56 Tien Giang
57 Tra Vinh
58 Tuyen Quang
59 Vinh Long
60 Vinh Phuc
61 Yen Bai

Annamese
  Cordillera
  B2–B3

Cambodia A4–C4
Central
  Highlands C4
China A1–D2

Da Lat C4
Dien Bien Phu A1

Fan Si Pan-Sa
  Phin (mountain
  range) B1

Gulf of Thailand
  A4–B5
Gulf of Tonkin
  B2–C2

Ha Long Bay C1
Haiphong C1
Hanoi B1
Ho Chi Minh City
  (Saigon) C5
Hue C3

Lang Son C1
Laos A1–C4

Mekong River
  A1–C5

Mount Fan Si
  Pan B1
Myanmar
  (Burma) A1

Nha Trang C4

Qui Nhon C4
Red River A1–C2
South China Sea
  D1–C5

Thailand A2–B4

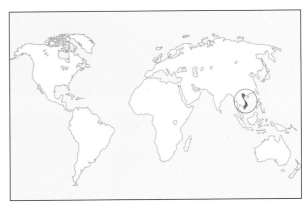

Quick Facts

Official Name	Socialist Republic of Vietnam
Capital	Hanoi
Official Language	Vietnamese
Population	81,098,416 (2002 estimate)
Land Area	127,243 square miles (329,560 square km)
Highest Point	Mount Fan Si Pan 10,312 feet (3,143 m)
Major Rivers	Mekong, Red
Main Religions	Buddhism, Roman Catholicism, Protestantism, Islam, Hoa Hao, Cao Dai
Major Festivals	Tet (January/February) Mid-Autumn Festival (September)
National Holidays	Independence Day (September 2) Liberation Day (April 30)
Currency	Vietnamese Dong (VND 15,297 = U.S. $1 as of 2002)

Opposite: This tower built by the Cham people is near Nha Trang.

Glossary

bronze: a type of metal that is made by mixing copper and tin.

communist: related to a political system in which the government owns and controls all of the nation's goods and resources.

Confucianism: an ancient Chinese philosophy, based on the teachings of Confucius, emphasizing social harmony, respect for authority, and responsibility to both family and community.

cycle: a series of events that keep repeating in the same order.

da cau (dah cow)**:** a game in which players kick a shuttlecock back and forth over a net, trying to keep it from touching the ground.

dynasty: a family of rulers who inherit their power.

ethnic groups: cultures of people who have the same heritage and customs.

fled: ran away to escape from danger.

inlay: patterns of decorative material set into the surface of another material.

intellectuals: people whose work requires study and high intelligence.

karaoke: a form of entertainment in which people sing along to recorded music.

merchants: people who make a living by buying, selling, or trading goods, or merchandise.

monosyllabic: made up of words that have only one unit of speech.

municipalities: cities or towns that have their own local governments.

mythical: belonging to a legend or an imaginary story.

nationalist: a person who is loyal and devoted to his or her home country.

offerings: gifts that are presented as a form of worship.

persecuted: treated cruelly because of background, beliefs, or behaviors.

policy: an official plan or rule that guides actions and decisions.

prose: writing in the form of ordinary speech, rather than poetry.

script: written, rather than printed, lettering that looks like handwriting.

submissive: willing to be controlled by others.

timber: wood that is used for building.

tones: voice sounds with distinct qualities, such as pitch or vibration.

typhoons: violent tropical storms in Pacific regions.

views: ways of thinking; opinions.

More Books to Read

Children of the Dragon: Selected Tales from Vietnam. Sherry Garland (Harcourt)

Children of Vietnam. The World's Children series. Marybeth Lorbiecki (Carolrhoda Books)

A Family from Vietnam. Families Around the World series. Simon Scoones (Raintree/Steck-Vaughn)

Leaving Vietnam: The True Story of Tuan Ngo. Sarah S. Kilborne (Econo-Clad Books)

The People of Vietnam. Celebrating the Peoples and Civilizations of Southeast Asia series. Dolly Brittan (Powerkids Press)

Vietnam. Countries of the World series. Michael S. Dahl (Bridgestone Books)

Vietnam. Festivals of the World series. Susan McKay (Gareth Stevens)

Water Buffalo Days: Growing Up in Vietnam. Huynh Quang Nhuong (HarperCollins Children's Books)

Videos

American Cultures for Children: Vietnamese-American Heritage. (Schlessinger Media)

Living in Vietnam. (Library Video)

Lonely Planet: The Vietnam Experience. (Questar)

Windows to the World: Vietnam. (Questar)

Web Sites

www.oxfam.org.uk/coolplanet/kidsweb/world/vietnam/viethome.htm

www.pbs.org/hitchhikingvietnam/life/core.html

www.timeforkids.com/TFK/specials/0,6709,187312,00.html

www.vietnamembassy-usa.org/learn/

Due to the dynamic nature of the Internet, some web sites stay current longer than others. To find additional web sites, use a reliable search engine with one or more of the following keywords to help you locate information about Vietnam. Keywords: *Ha Long Bay, Hanoi, Ho Chi Minh, Mekong River, Saigon, water puppets.*

Index